John Calvin: Spread of the Reformation

By Richard L. Harrison, Jr.

Contents

1

The Reformation Re-formed

The Reformation movement was barely underway when other Christians began to raise questions similar to those raised by Martin Luther. These people also wanted to seek ways to renew the life of the church. One such person was Ulrich Zwingli (1484–1531), a Swiss patriot and powerful preacher.

Like Luther, Zwingli was distressed over the worldliness of the church. He was dismayed that the salvation the crucified Christ offered was being sold for various amounts of gold. As Luther had done, Zwingli turned to the Scriptures. He used the new tools Christian scholars developed to study the Bible and began to translate the original Greek and Hebrew languages of Scripture into the sturdy, direct phrases of Swiss German.

January 1, 1519, was Zwingli's first Sunday as preacher in the main church of Zurich. This church was known as the Great Minster. He startled the congregation by announcing that he intended to begin a series of sermons based on the New Testament. Zwingli started with Matthew 1 and promised to pick up the next Sunday where he had left off, gradually working his way through the entire New Testament. His teaching style of preaching captured the imagination of the people, and they were eager to hear and learn more.

Zwingli represents an example of how the Renaissance contributed to the Reformation. From such thinkers as Erasmus (1466–1536), Zwingli learned the importance of studying Scripture in Greek and Hebrew. When Zwingli preached, he read, translating directly from the Greek New Testament that Erasmus had published. Zwingli also appreciated Erasmus's concept of the "philosophy of Christ," that is, using the simple teachings of Jesus as a guide for living. This way of understanding Christ led Zwingli to be critical of the power and wealth of many of the people in the church.

A few months after arriving in Zurich, Zwingli became ill with a plague. He apparently caught the dangerous disease when he offered pastoral comfort to the sick and dying. He came close to death, and his life's direction was changed. Prior to this illness, much of his motivation came from his intellectual commitment to the righteousness and justness of the Reformation cause. Afterward, however, he found himself living with a new understanding of the power of God's grace.

The writings of the apostle Paul took on a profound significance for Zwingli. He began to see life as being in the hands of God. Zwingli came to believe that God had chosen him for a special task. Henceforth, Zwingli would teach a strong doctrine of predestination.

About this time Zwingli also learned of Luther's activities and may have read a good bit of Luther's writings. On the one hand, Zwingli realized that Luther was a kindred spirit. On the other, a certain rivalry seemed to erupt between Zwingli and Luther. Neither Zwingli nor Luther wanted to admit any influence or direction from the other. This rivalry would lead to division, bitter words, and harsh accusations.

For the moment, however, Zwingli's preaching excited the people of Zurich and the surrounding region. The leaders of Zurich looked to Ulrich Zwingli for guidance in directing the life of the church in the city.

Zwingli appealed to a sense of patriotism that was arising among the Swiss. He was concerned that various foreign powers were hiring Swiss men to be mercenaries. Years earlier, Zwingli had accompanied Swiss troops to Italy, serving as a chaplain. He saw young Swiss men slaughtered in the name of territorial conflict between French and Italian factions. Zwingli understood that a declining economy and resulting unemployment had led many Swiss men to offer themselves to the highest bidder.

Zwingli's reformation of the church thus became intertwined with his call for a stronger Switzerland. He wanted Swiss soldiers to serve Swiss needs. He wanted the towns and cities to become stronger and to provide jobs for everyone who could work. In the minds of many of the Swiss followers of Zwingli, the Reformation became a reform of church *and* society. To oppose the religious Reformation was to be unpatriotic.

But other Swiss Christians believed that one could be a faithful Swiss and a good Roman Catholic and that the Reformation was a part of an attempt by some of the stronger cities to dominate the rural regions. Like the German Reformation, the Swiss Reformation was intertwined with conflicting views of patriotism and nationalism.

Introduction of the Reformation to Zurich

During the years 1523–1525, Zwingli engaged in a series of debates with Roman Catholic defenders of the papacy. With each debate the Zurich City Council moved closer to establishing the Reformation and breaking ties with Rome. Zwingli's success as a debater was reinforced by his preaching and teaching. He brought other reform-minded ministers and teachers to work with him, and the people responded positively. At one point, in a city of some six thousand people, over two hundred ministers and teachers labored to bring about the Reformation.

By 1525, the members of the city council ordered an end to the celebration of Mass in Zurich. They replaced it with an austere form of worship. Zwingli had come to believe that the New Testament was a clear guide to faith and to church practice, and only that which the New Testament expressly commanded or offered as an example was to be followed in the church.

For this reason, the people of Zurich observed the Lord's Supper as a starkly simple rite. The worshipers gathered about a table instead of coming before an altar. Prayers were offered. Then the bread was broken and the wine poured and passed from person to person. No choirs sang anthems and choral responses to the Mass. Instead, the congregation sang psalms. And the congregation sang without the accompaniment of organs or other musical instruments, for none are mentioned in the New Testament. (Zwingli was an accomplished musician and could play several instruments. He never opposed the use of musical instruments in the home or in other non-church settings.)

Statues, paintings, and stained glass windows were removed from churches. Zwingli and his followers regarded these works of art as idols corrupting the faith of the people. Zwingli felt their use was a violation of the commandment against graven images. The response to Zwingli's ideas was so great that on numerous occasions he found himself having to urge the people to effect change only through legal channels and not through riots.

Zwingli and Luther

In many ways Zwingli's approach was a more extreme form of the Reformation than that of Luther, and it was based on a more radical understanding of the nature and purpose of Scripture. Luther taught that at those points where Scripture was silent, the

5

general spirit of Scripture, reason, tradition, and a clear conscience could guide the church. Luther called for a more modest reform of worship than that which Zwingli offered.

This disagreement was what led Zwingli and Luther to a separation. Zwingli's rejection of the Roman Catholic Mass included an even more vigorous opposition to the Roman interpretation of the Mass than Luther's rejection of it. Luther believed that in the Lord's Supper the body and blood of Jesus were truly and actually offered to the worshiper along with the bread and the wine. Zwingli taught that Jesus was *symbolically* present for the faithful believer.

Luther thought that Zwingli's interpretation denied a crucial aspect of the teaching of Jesus and that it denied the continuing presence of the Lord. Beginning in 1525, Luther and Zwingli began to debate in print and in sermons. Their allies and coworkers in the Reformation found themselves taking sides. The sense of rivalry between the two leaders of the Reformation showed itself to be deep-seated and rooted as much in a desire for control as in strongly held beliefs.

This controversy occurred at the very time that the Reformation was growing and gaining strength, a time when Emperor Charles V was unable to use force against Protestant preachers, princes, and cities. Some Protestant leaders realized that the situation could change rapidly, but the Protestants were still too small a group to take on the great strength of the emperor and other political leaders who remained loyal to the church of Rome. One of these Protestant leaders, Philip of Hesse, and Martin Bucer (pronounced BOOT-zer), a leading Protestant preacher in Strasbourg, called for a meeting between Luther and Zwingli. They hoped that such a conference could lead to a reconciliation between the giants of the Reformation, thus presenting a united front to the opponents of their cause.

In October 1529, Martin Luther and Ulrich Zwingli met face to face for the first time. Brought together at the castle of Philip of Hesse at Marburg in central Germany, they talked, debated, argued, pled for unity, and were able to agree on fourteen of fifteen points. However, they could not come to terms on the meaning of the Lord's Supper. They did accept a proposal to refrain from attacking each other, and the spirit of hostility was reduced for a short while.

Growth of Zwingli's Influence

Meanwhile, throughout southern Germany and Switzerland and in many of the cities of the upper Rhine Valley, Protestants were turning to Zwingli and the Swiss Reformation for leadership. The church leaders in the important trading city of Strasbourg were especially inclined to do so. Martin Bucer and Wolfgang Capito had introduced the Reformation there, first under the inspiration of Martin Luther but with increasing attention given to Zwingli's ideas. Bucer and Capito were particularly concerned to see the whole community shaped by Christian values. These persons knew that the form and structure of worship would be a significant force in directing the outlook and character of the Christian community.

The Strasbourg reformers also continued to work for unity among Protestants after the limited success of the meeting at Marburg. Their desire for unity was based on more than just a fear of weakness brought about by division. They believed that division in the church was wrong, that the Christian community should be characterized by love and patience, and that there should be some level of toleration of differences of opinion.

In 1530, Emperor Charles V returned to the Holy Roman Empire (the heart of which was Germany). He wanted to settle the dispute over religion. The followers of Luther prepared a statement of faith to be presented to the emperor and to the Imperial Diet (a kind of parliament) at its meeting in Augsburg. At first the south German cities wanted to be able to sign a common document with the Lutherans and thus present a united front. But the followers of Luther used the occasion to present a document that was both very Lutheran and at the same time conciliatory toward Rome on some issues.

The Protestants whom Zwingli influenced could not accept the Lutherans' position. So, they presented a statement of their own. They had hoped that Zwingli would join them in the writing of a confession of faith and that Zurich would be one of the cities signing the confession. But Zwingli wanted nothing to do with the process, in large measure because the Swiss wanted to preserve their independence from the Empire. Four of the south German cities agreed on an affirmation of faith that Martin Bucer wrote. This *Tetrapolitana*, "Four Cities" statement, became one of the earliest confessions of faith for the "re-formed" Protestants.

The Radical Reformation

The Lutherans and the Reformed were not the only early examples of Protestantism. The fracturing of the church soon resulted in numerous movements, most of which both the Lutherans and the Reformed bitterly opposed. Late in 1521, some radical visionaries had visited Wittenberg. The unsettling effect of their visit had led to Luther's early return from exile. Then, in 1524–1525, the bloody and costly Peasants' War erupted throughout much of Germany. Many of the revolutionaries included the reform of religion among their demands for change in society.

Then, at about the same time, some of the followers of Zwingli in Zurich urged him to go further than he was willing to go. Felix Manz and Conrad Grebel were both well educated. They were among Zwingli's early supporters. Manz and Grebel participated in Bible study groups, and through their study they came to believe that infant baptism had no basis in the New Testament.

The issue was not merely the practice of baptizing

people of a certain age but was even more a concern about the nature of the Christian community. Manz and Grebel thought infant baptism was indiscriminate, merely a social practice. They thought infant baptism made the church simply an extension of the secular community. Manz and Grebel argued that the church should be the community of the faithful. Therefore, only those able to show that they had accepted the Christian faith for themselves should be baptized and added to the church.

Zwingli at first expressed some interest in Manz and Grebel's ideas, for clearly all baptized church members were not Christians in their practices and beliefs. The idea of the church as the loyal and faithful community, even though it might well be a minority of a community, was intriguing. But as Zwingli reflected further, he realized that the biblical basis for such a radical change was less than absolutely clear.

Furthermore, all relationships in society (all areas related to marriage and to the signing of contracts, all political alliances, all expressions of civic loyalty) were based on oaths sworn by Christians. If some citizens were not baptized, which would surely be the result if the church abandoned infant baptism, then the whole structure of society would be threatened. There would be no sure and accountable basis for either economic or political life. That was more than Zwingli was willing to risk.

The Anabaptists

Zwingli entered into dialogue with the growing group of radicals in Zurich. In January 1525, after a public debate, the city council concluded that Zwingli had proven his point and that Grebel and Manz were to be silent about the issue in public. A couple of their more outspoken colleagues were banished from the city.

The radicals responded by meeting in private, and they began to practice believers' baptism. Since all of these people had been baptized as infants, they began to be called rebaptizers, or *Anabaptists*. To the Anabaptists, however, their baptism as infants had been no baptism at all. By the end of January 1525, a congregation of some thirty-five Anabaptists had formed. These persons began refusing to have their newborn children baptized; this led to a public confrontation with city authorities. Punishments were meted out, and some of the Anabaptists were sent into exile. The movement spread with astonishing rapidity.

The first Anabaptists in Zurich were educated middle and upper-class persons. As a movement, however, the Anabaptists appealed most to the lower classes, to those who were on the underside of wealth and power in society. The expression of radical ideas seemed to give birth to yet more radical ideas. Within a few years groups of radical Christians, some of them Anabaptist but many not, were to be found in many parts of Europe.

Some of these radical Christians urged the formation of communal societies. Others simply asked to be left alone to live their faith and lives in peace. But for the established powers of the day, such digressions from the norm were unheard of and posed a threat. As a result, in a short time Protestant and Roman Catholic authorities were executing religious radicals. In Zurich some Anabaptists were executed by drowning, a death that ridiculed the radicals' practice of baptism by immersion.

A truly serious outbreak of revolutionary radicalism occurred in the northwestern German city of Munster in 1534 and 1535. A group of mentally unbalanced extremists overthrew the government and established a reign of terror. By the time they were defeated and executed, all radicals were tarnished with a brush dipped in the blood of Munster. However, the vast majority of religious radicals and virtually all Anabaptists were not only appalled by the violence of Munster but were themselves pacifists who would not resist authorities who harrassed them.

The Anabaptists' cause began to take a more

positive turn when a Dutch priest named Menno Simons (1496–1561) was converted to their way of thinking. His effective and capable leadership led many of the Anabaptists to take on his name and call themselves Mennonites.

Zwingli's Final Conflict

The waters swirling around the reformers was muddied all the more by the internal political and religious strife in Switzerland. In October 1531, the people of the Roman Catholic regions near Zurich sought to regain some of the prestige that they had lost in conflicts with Zurich and the Protestants. The issues were economic and political as well as religious.

Word came to Zurich that a Roman Catholic army was marching on the city. The call to arms was given, and some thirty preachers joined the other citizens in going out to meet the threat. In the mountain fields and meadows near Kappel, south of Zurich, Swiss Protestant met Swiss Catholic. The rapidly deployed Zurichers ran into a disciplined and well-prepared army. By the end of the battle the rural Roman Catholics had won a decisive victory over the urban Protestants.

For centuries Protestant legends told of the martyrdom of Zwingli. People said that, serving as a chaplain, he knelt down by a fallen compatriot to offer comfort and solace. Then suddenly from behind a battle ax dealt the reformer a deadly blow. However, more recent research indicates that Zwingli the patriot died as a combatant with weapon in hand. His enemies cut his body into pieces and then burned them.

After this battle, one of the first major armed conflicts between Protestants and Roman Catholics, the defeated citizens of Zurich went back to their city to lick their wounds and to rebuild. Zwingli's wife received a harsh message. Her husband, a son, her brother, and a brother-in-law were all killed in defense of the faith.

When Luther heard of Zwingli's death, he commented brusquely that all who live by the sword die by the sword. He believed that the judgment of God was at work in the death of his Swiss rival.

The Reformed Protestants Continue

Zwingli was replaced by his son-in-law, the stalwart Heinrich Bullinger (1504–1575). For the next fifty years he protected the memory and work of Zwingli in Zurich and beyond.

Despite Zwingli's death, the Protestants who had looked to him for leadership continued to offer a direction for the Protestant cause that differed from Luther's. Quite some time would pass before Bullinger would exercise effective leadership outside of Switzerland. Martin Bucer of Strasbourg was the most active leader of Protestants in the region, but his deep desire for Protestant unity had marked him as perhaps untrustworthy in dealings with Luther. Some of Zwingli's followers feared that Bucer was willing to give up too much in the quest for unity.

Nevertheless, this "re-formed" Reformation continued to grow and to expand. The movement was particularly strong in the towns and cities of Germany and Switzerland and was appearing in areas of France as well as in the Netherlands.

We need to be aware that in the beginning the Reformation was largely an urban movement. Zwingli was deeply involved with Zurich. Bucer was deeply involved with Strasbourg. The urban setting of and urban support for the Reformation were the key to the initial success and survival of the Protestant cause.

After a few years the cities would decline in importance, especially in Lutheran circles, and be replaced by powerful princes. But for the "re-formed" Protestantism led by Zwingli, and later by John Calvin, the urban areas were both the center of activity and the base of operations. The Reformation was usually a partnership betweeen the church and the government of the city. The church had authority over preaching and teaching. The city government generally had control over enforcement of doctrine and morals and administered some church funds and property.

Cities had a long history of struggling to maintain some independence from both church and national secular rulers. Many city dwellers readily accepted the Reformation message with its call to clean up abuses in the church. In most cases this acceptance occurred among the lower-class artisans and then among the middle-class merchants. Because the Reformation was a popular movement with popular support, city councils (made up of mostly wealthier citizens) would listen and slowly give in to the demands for change. Separating self-interest from genuine conviction as the reason city leaders agreed to bring in the Reformation is difficult, if not impossible. Most individuals and groups had trouble resisting a movement that appealed to their ideals and also offered the possibility of enhanced power and wealth.

At the same time, however, the civic leaders understood quite well the dangers of going against the established church. At any time the emperor could find himself in control of his far-flung territories and turn with power and force to restore order and the traditional church within the borders of the Holy Roman Empire. While self-interest was sometimes involved in city council decisions, deep conviction and courage were also present.

However, with no dominant leader, with no one person fully trusted to give direction and shape to the Reformed movement, the danger clearly existed that Lutheran opponents or Roman Catholic political strength could undermine or even destroy the efforts of these reform-minded people. They needed a leader.

2

A Leader Is Born, and Made

Northeast of Paris, near the junction of the Verse and Oise rivers, set in the midst of rolling fields and hedgerows, is the old cathedral town of Noyon. This region of Picardy has seen much history. Even little Noyon was once the setting for high political drama. Charlemagne was crowned "King of All the Franks" there. But for five hundred years after the millennial year of A.D. 1000, Noyon lived a quiet life. No one noticed when another son was born to Gerard and Jeanne Cauvin, or Calvin, on July 10, 1509.

Calvin's Early Life and Education

John Calvin was born into a family that was ambitious and quite eager to become more prosperous and respected in Noyon and in the surrounding countryside. Gerard was a financial officer for the cathedral. He made sure that his sons were educated, and he helped arrange for his bright son John to spend time in the household of one of the most prominent noble families in the region. In that setting John studied with the noble children and their tutor and had an opportunity to learn the manners and ways of the powerful of this world.

With such connections in the church and in the community, Gerard Calvin made the necessary arrangements for John to pursue a career in the church. This career would mean university education and a series of positions that would bring wealth and prestige to John and to his family.

John's career as a "minister" began when he was not quite twelve. At that time he was made a chaplain of one of the chapels in the cathedral. Such appointments had been a church practice for many years. The position was funded by the income from land or from other investments. The person given the position would use some of the income to pay a poor priest to fulfill the basic obligations of the office. The person would then use the rest of the income for himself. In this way some people could become wealthy by amassing numerous church offices and positions, while paying small amounts to substitute priests. Church officeholders did not even have to become ordained priests. However, John was admitted to a lower level of clergy at the age of twelve. Over the next few years John's father arranged for several of these positions. He used them to pay for John's education.

John was probably no more than twelve when he left the security of little Noyon and traveled to Paris to become a student at the University of Paris. In those days going to the university at a young age was not at all unusual, for the university encompassed what would now include everything after grammar school. The University of Paris was one of the grandest of all universities in the sixteenth century and had the reputation for both excellence and orthodoxy in its theology curriculum. Teachers at Paris followed the straight and narrow of church doctrine.

Most of Calvin's early course work concentrated on improving his knowledge of Latin, for that was the language of all teaching and learning in the universities of that day. Until students mastered Latin, they could not advance toward a degree.

Calvin's main Latin teacher was one who would later be accused of being a Protestant. No evidence exists to prove that this teacher was an advocate of the Reformation at the time of Calvin's work with him. However, this teacher probably already held at that time the sentiments that would later cause him to support the Protestant cause.

John Calvin worked hard. The curriculum was rigorous, emphasizing the traditional ways of learning and understanding. Few advocates of the Renaissance were on the faculty, and certainly no one taught the ideas and values of humanism. But Calvin, like many of the students, was eager to study the new ideas; he seems to have sought out those who wanted to be able to express modern ways of thinking.

Calvin transferred from one college to another in order to advance his preparation for work in the church. In the College de Montaigu (a part of the University of Paris), Calvin found himself in one of the most conservative of all the schools in the city. Years before, the young Erasmus, the great Renaissance humanist, had experienced the tough and narrow perspective of Montaigu. (Soon after Calvin moved on, another student would arrive, one who responded more postively to the direction of the school: Ignatius Loyola. He was the future founder of the Jesuits, the primary Roman Catholic organization that preached against Protestantism.)

About the time that Calvin finished the equivalent of his undergraduate education, perhaps about 1526, he received word from his father that he was to change direction and study law. Apparently, Calvin's father found himself in conflict with the priests who administered the cathedral in Noyon. He was accused of financial mismanagement at least, and in the course of controversy he became bitter about the way the cathedral priests treated him. So, he directed Calvin to look elsewhere for a career.

John moved to Orléans because the university there was far stronger than Paris in the study of law. Calvin worked diligently and pushed himself to excel. He worked hard at developing his memory, a discipline that would pay dividends in years to come. But he spent part of his time in what for him was a new direction, the study of classical literature, that is, the writings of the ancient Greeks and Romans. The spirit of the Renaissance was blooming in Orléans, and Calvin reveled in the freedom of thought and new approaches to learning.

Calvin's experience of the Renaissance was even more pronounced the next year when he transferred to the University of Bourges. Even though Calvin continued to study law, Bourges offered far more opportunities to study the literature and languages of the ancients. His Greek teacher was but one of several teachers at Bourges who later would be known for their support of the Reformation.

Calvin's father died in 1531, thus freeing Calvin to pursue his own interests. After receiving his law degree early the next year, Calvin turned his attention to literature. He returned briefly to Paris. Change was clearly in the wind there. King Francis I was supporting the appointment of Renaissance humanists to the faculty.

Calvin's Conversion to Protestantism

Calvin became a part of a circle of young Renaissance scholars and teachers. These people were daring and exciting. They were the avant-garde, the cutting edge of intellectual and cultural life in one of the great cities of Europe.

From 1532 to 1533, Calvin lived in Paris off and on. He sometimes traveled to other cities, alternating between his life as a scholar and his life as a lawyer. His legal activities probably served to finance his literary endeavors. We know little about this time in his life. However, almost certainly during this period he began to move strongly, definitely, toward Protestantism.

One of Calvin's closest friends, Nicholas Cop, had recently been elected Rector of the University of Paris, an office filled with more work than honor. Cop gave his inaugural address in October 1533. During this address he dared to quote from Luther and argued a clearly Protestant position.

As a result, Cop had to flee Paris for his life. Calvin went with him. Calvin's room was searched. The life of the scholar had become filled with danger.

Calvin spent the next several months in travel. He enjoyed the stimulating companionship of other humanists and reformers in the region of Angouleme.

By this time Calvin was most likely a convinced Protestant. According to tradition, he celebrated the Lord's Supper in a cave near Poitiers. He used a large slab of rock as a Communion table. He began to write theological works that showed he was well advanced in his Protestant views.

In the fall of 1534, French Protestants found themselves in a significantly more dangerous position. During the night of October 18, some Protestant daredevils placed posters all over Paris calling for support of the Protestant cause. They put one poster on the inner door of the royal bedroom. The king was furious and fearful that agents of revolution could get so close to him. This "Affair of the Placards" resulted in the arrest of hundreds of Protestants. Thirty-five people were burned at the stake. Among those killed was Calvin's brother Charles.

The Life of an Exile

Even Angouleme became a dangerous place to live. Calvin had to move; he had to leave France. He settled in Basel, Switzerland, where he lived quietly and wrote and met several Protestant leaders. Among these persons was Heinrich Bullinger, Zwingli's successor in Zurich. In 1536, Calvin published the first edition of his *Institutes of the Christian Religion*, his most famous work (of which more will be said later). He dedicated the book to King Francis I and called on him to stop persecuting God's people.

Right after the publication of the *Institutes*, Calvin

and his friend Louis de Tillet traveled to Ferrara in Italy to visit the court of Duchess Renée d'Este. Just why Calvin made the trip is not certain. Some scholars have speculated that he went there to encourage her to become a public supporter of the Reformation. However, while in Ferrara, Calvin saw the aggressive power of the loyal Roman Catholics at work. Protestants were being arrested despite protection by the duchess.

The trip was important for Calvin. He was able to meet more Protestants, both in Ferrara and on the way to and from the city. He also became even more aware of the terrible price some people were paying for their new beliefs.

Calvin returned to Basel and then headed for Paris. The fickle nature of political alliances made France safe for a while. King Francis I was involved in a war with the Holy Roman Emperor, Charles V, and Francis wanted to have some of the Protestant princes of Germany as allies against their own emperor. So, the persecution of Protestants was interrupted.

The Call From Geneva

Calvin was looking forward to living a quiet life as a writer in behalf of the Protestant cause. His book, the *Institutes*, had announced to the world that a new, profoundly capable defender of the Reformation was on the scene. Bucer and other ministers in Strasbourg had arranged for Calvin to receive an income, so he planned to move there.

The war between Francis I and Charles V blocked the direct route from Paris to Strasbourg. Calvin knew about this situation before he began his trip. So, he took a long, roundabout way that sent him southeast, through Geneva. While Calvin was spending the evening in Geneva, someone recognized him and informed the leaders of the Reformation in Geneva about his presence.

For centuries Geneva had been under the control of its bishop, and the bishops of Geneva had generally been members of the House of Savoy. Savoy had sought to maintain direct or indirect control of Geneva. When the citizens of Geneva began a serious movement to free themselves from their medieval overlords, this process caused them to challenge both church and state.

The Swiss city of Bern supported the Genevans in this drive for independence. Bern was already strongly and evangelistically Protestant by 1530. As a result, Protestant preachers began to have the opportunity to work in Geneva at that time. In 1535, the City Council of Geneva proclaimed an end to the celebration of the Mass and in its place instituted the official observance of Reformed worship. Political maneuvering continued, and Duke Charles II of Savoy renewed his war with Geneva. Bern challenged the duke but also argued that Geneva must become subservient to Bern.

In the midst of siege and war and troop movements, with threats, counterthreats, alliances, betrayals, cowardice, and courage all around, somehow Geneva emerged from the conflict in the spring of 1536 as an independent state. The city would remain independent for the next 250 years. Indeed, Geneva did not even join the Swiss Confederation until 1815.

The Genevans had already invited Guillaume (William) Farel to work for the Protestant cause in their city. Farel was an effective and powerful preacher. He had been at work in Geneva since 1532.

When Farel learned of the presence in Geneva of Calvin, the brilliant young defender of Protestantism, Farel was sure that God was at work. Farel had been praying for someone of extraordinary ability to help him in this difficult situation. He went immediately to the hotel to talk to Calvin.

Calvin felt flattered by Farel's invitation, but he was firm in his belief that he was called to a life of quiet scholarship. The arrangements had all been made, and Strasbourg, while not a French-speaking city, was much closer to his homeland of Picardy. Bucer was expecting him. No, Calvin could not remain.

However, Farel would not accept a negative response. He pleaded, he cajoled, and then he threatened. He threatened Calvin with the only weapon that would undo Calvin: the will of God. The red-bearded Farel thundered that God had obviously sent Calvin to Geneva to join in the Reformation there; and if Calvin fled this call of God, he would know firsthand the righteous indignation of the Almighty.

Calvin agreed to stay. Much later he observed, "William Farel detained me at Geneva, not so much by counsel and exhortation, as by a dreadful imprecation, which I felt to be as if God had from heaven laid his mighty hand upon me to arrest me."[1] Calvin reported that Farel had also said that "God would curse my retirement, and the tranquility of the studies which I sought. . . . I was so stricken with terror, that I desisted from the journey which I had undertaken."[2]

Calvin's First Efforts in Geneva

Geneva was a city of substance when John Calvin stopped over in that July of 1536. With some ten thousand citizens, Geneva was larger by far than any city for miles around. While its annual fair no longer drew the crowds that had made the city famous and prosperous in the late Middle Ages, Geneva continued to have a steady and fundamentally sound economy. Geneva had all that was required to become a significant base of operations for a religious revolution. All that was needed was to organize the city according to Reformation principles.

Like Bucer, Calvin believed that Christians were under obligation not only to preach and teach the truth but also to live it. Christians were to try to create a community that was guided by, inspired by, and led by the vision of God's will. Farel and Calvin knew that in order to reform the community, they must first fully organize the church.

In January 1537, Calvin and Farel presented to the Small Council of Geneva a proposal for the church: *Articles Concerning the Organization of the Church and of*

Worship at Geneva. This proposal was a plan for the complete reformation of the church. The plan called for observance of the Lord's Supper each Sunday and stated that only the "worthy" should be allowed to partake of the bread and wine. While the city council permitted only a quarterly celebration, it did accept the other provisions for maintaining the sanctity of the Lord's Supper, including procedures to examine all citizens to determine whether they should be admitted to Communion.

Both for the preservation of the purity of the Lord's Supper and as a way of building a Christian community, the *Articles* called for the appointment of monitors in each section of the city. These persons were to observe their neighbors and report on any sins committed. The sinners were to be brought before the ministers who would encourage repentance and a change of heart. If that attempt did not work, the sinners would be excommunicated.

Calvin also wrote a little book in which he summarized the primary Protestant doctrines: *Instruction in Faith*. This book, along with a *Confession of Faith for Geneva*, revealed a Reformation that was rooted in the authority of the Bible with Scripture as the rule and guide for faith and for the church. Calvin expressed the classic Protestant concerns with clarity and with brevity, including salvation by faith through grace, the sacraments of baptism and the Lord's Supper as visible avenues of grace, and the Protestant view of church and ministry. The two documents affirmed the authority of the rulers of the world, whether city authorities or princes and kings.

Resistance to Reform

Under the leadership of Calvin and Farel, the city council decreed that all citizens were to make a public oath accepting the *Confession of Faith*. Those persons who refused to do so would no longer be church members and thus would no longer have the rights of citizenship in the city. Many people opposed the plan, and the magistrates were hesitant in announcing and carrying out penalties for failure to make the necessary oaths.

Many citizens felt they had just overthrown the heavy hand of the bishop and of the House of Savoy. They wanted nothing to do with a new set of power holders, even if they were Protestant ministers. Other people were concerned that by not following the Protestant order as established in Bern, Geneva would be in danger of alienating her new and critically important ally.

On February 4, 1538, an election took place that changed the balance of power in the various city councils. Conflict soon erupted between the ministers and the city rulers. Farel and Calvin were ordered to cease preaching. They refused and were sent into exile on April 23.

Both Farel and Calvin were angry and frustrated. Both "shook off the dust from [their] feet" (Matthew 10:14) and moved on. After attending a meeting of Protestant leaders in Zurich, Farel went back to his beloved Neuchatel and served there for the rest of his life. Calvin decided that this situation was the opportunity he needed to pick up where he had left off just two years prior. An invitation from Basel lay before him. So, he followed the Rhine to that lovely and gracious city, a place where he was a welcome guest and coworker.

Calvin thought that in Basel the quiet life of a scholar would finally be his. After Geneva, Calvin craved peace. He had been shaken by his failure to achieve his goals in Geneva. But in Basel he could settle down and write. His study would be his pulpit. At least, so he thought.

---

[1] From "Preface to the Commentary on the Book of Psalms," by John Calvin, in *John Calvin: Selections From His Writings,* edited by John Dillenberger (Scholars Press, 1975); page 28.

[2] From *John Calvin: Selections From His Writings*; page 28.

3

Calvin and His Reformation Mature

Calvin in Strasbourg

No sooner had Calvin arrived in Basel than Martin Bucer in Strasbourg began writing him. Bucer urged Calvin to come a little farther north, a little farther along the Rhine to Strasbourg. Bucer said that much work needed to be done, and Calvin was the one to do it.

Calvin's timid character had been deeply scarred by his failure to succeed in Geneva. The idea of beginning another public ministry was loathsome to him. No, Calvin wanted to be a scholar and to write for the church and for the good of the kingdom of God.

Bucer would not take no for an answer. Along with other preachers and civic leaders of Strasbourg, Bucer argued that Calvin could follow his scholarly career in Strasbourg while also assisting in ministry to the French-speaking refugees there. In that way Calvin could assist the Reformation in France. Calvin still resisted.

Then Bucer, following the lead of Farel, challenged Calvin with the threat that God was calling him to come to Strasbourg. The request to come to Strasbourg was not merely his friend Martin seeking to have him as a coworker and companion. No, God had prepared Calvin for the work at hand in Strasbourg. If Calvin refused to come, Bucer said that he would be another Jonah, fleeing from God's will, fleeing from God's righteous opportunity for service; and the consequences would be most serious for Calvin's soul. Calvin trembled before the threat of God's wrath and accepted the invitation. Fortunately, Strasbourg provided a welcome sojourn for John Calvin. In contrast to his experience in Geneva, in Strasbourg, Calvin was among friends. The city authorities were clearly behind the Reformation. People encouraged Calvin to take time to reflect and write and teach. Calvin felt needed there.

Strasbourg was a jewel of a city. It was a place where people had welcomed the Reformation as early as 1524. The city council had supported various Protestant preachers, the most prominent of whom was Martin Bucer. The secular leader of the city was Jacob Sturm, a man of learning and vision. He led the city to develop schools for people of all ages. Working with Bucer, Sturm instituted a program of education that ultimately evolved into a system from kindergarten through university studies.

Strasbourg was a city that had opened its doors to refugees of all kinds, including many radical reformers (particularly Anabaptists, so long as they maintained the peace and did not disrupt the social order). Among the refugees were some five hundred French Protestants who had been without a preacher for some time. In September 1538, Calvin began his work with his fellow French.

A few months later, Calvin was asked to give regular public lectures as a part of the community education program that the city and the church were developing. Calvin found himself either preaching or lecturing virtually every day. While this schedule was quite demanding, it also gave him direction in his scholarship; and he brought to conclusion a commentary on the Book of Romans.

Calvin would eventually publish commentaries on all but eleven books of the Old Testament and on all of the books of the New Testament except Revelation (he often said that Revelation was beyond him; he claimed he could not understand it).

Guided by Bucer, Calvin developed a structure for worship that would serve as a model for his teaching on worship throughout his career. As he had done in Geneva, Calvin sought to institute weekly Communion, but the city magistrates approved only a monthly observance. He added parts of the Ten Commandments to the Sunday service, often sung by the congregation; and he made use of a number of traditional prayers and responses altered to reflect Protestant beliefs.

Calvin's personal life changed radically during his sojourn in Strasbourg. Up to that time Calvin had not expressed any interest in marriage. With his having been raised for a career in the church (which would have included a vow of celibacy), the dangers that had surrounded much of his initial Protestant activity, and his shy character, he seems to have had little interest in having a family.

Calvin's quieter, more regular, and settled life in Strasbourg might have turned his mind to marriage. Just as big an influence, perhaps more so, was the fact that Martin Bucer was a great promoter of matrimony.

Various friends tried to find a wife for Calvin. He came close to marriage first with a woman of noble birth and then with a woman who apparently had a more colorful reputation than Calvin could accept. He stated that he had simple intentions, desiring only that his wife "be modest, complaisant, unostentatious, thrifty, patient, and likely to be careful of my health." [1]

With Bucer's lively assistance, a proper match was finally made. In August 1540, Calvin married Idelette de Bure, a widow of an Anabaptist whom Calvin had converted to the mainstream Protestant position. Her husband had died during an outbreak of the plague. She brought with her a son and a daughter, both of whom Calvin treated as his own with affectionate and diligent care.

Two years later Idelette gave birth to a son, Jacques, who died shortly after coming into the world. The delivery damaged her health, and she was never to recover full strength. Her death in 1549 was an occasion for deep sorrow. While the marriage may have been anything but a romantic match, Calvin's comments and those of his friends clearly reveal that the relationship developed into one of great love.

A New Call From Geneva

All the time that Calvin lived and worked in Strasbourg, his supporters in Geneva struggled to have him recalled. A complicated political situation there prevented them from succeeding for several years. However, new circumstances in 1540 led the city council to write Calvin to ask him to return.

Calvin's response was polite (in public) but firm. He not only was happy in his work in Strasbourg, he thought of Geneva as a place where he had few friends, a place where he had made significant errors of judgment. Calvin was both angry about his treatment and embarrassed at what he believed to be his own inappropriate actions.

The Genevans then turned to Farel. While he would not return, he agreed to help them persuade Calvin to return. Farel began a letter-writing campaign not only to Calvin but also to Protestant leaders throughout Switzerland and southern Germany. The pressure mounted. The letters told Calvin that he must return and complete the task he had begun. Calvin resisted; and then Farel thundered again, threatening Calvin with divine judgment if he dared to resist the clear will of God. Calvin finally agreed to return to Geneva.

Reform in Geneva, Again

This time Calvin was in a much better position to reform the church as he saw fit. Not only had the city virtually begged him to come and lead the church, Calvin had also developed a broad reputation as a major personality in the Protestant movement. As such, he had much more personal authority than had been the case in 1536 when the minutes of the city council referred to him simply as "the Frenchman."

When Calvin resumed his place in the pulpit of the cathedral of Saint Peter, he preached from the same biblical text that had been his source for the last sermon he preached in Geneva just before he was ejected from the church and from the city. This beginning of his ministry provided a clear indication that Calvin would make no apologies for his earlier efforts and that the city could expect him to continue the same form of thorough reformation.

Calvin's first task was to write a kind of constitution for the church in Geneva. The first edition of these *Ecclesiastical Ordinances* appeared just a couple of weeks after he returned. He continued to revise them over the next twenty years. These ordinances formed the basis for the organization of churches that have to this day looked to Calvin for leadership, especially Reformed and Presbyterian churches.

The *Ordinances* provided for a fourfold structure of ministry, with pastors, teachers, elders, and deacons. Each had clearly delineated duties and responsibilities. The elders and deacons were from the laity; the pastors and teachers were ordained clergy. The elders joined the pastors in making up a consistory (or presbytery) that served as a primary governing board for the church.

The elders had a special responsibility for looking out for the moral welfare of the community. They would report to the consistory any infractions of church discipline, and the consistory could then take the appropriate action. The basic response from the consistory was usually a pastoral admonition and call for repentance. Continued infractions or very serious misdeeds could result in excommunication, and the consistory would turn the culprit over to the city council for appropriate punishment.

Maintenance of Discipline

This aspect of Calvin's Reformation has garnered the most attention over the years. Punishments were meted out for actions that people today would hardly notice. Certainly some actions that the consistory and magistrates took do seem quite extreme (especially the punishing of a man for naming his dog Calvin). But we need to be aware that what the Genevans did was to put into effect a kind of ideal that many people in that day held. Also, the result was the development of an extraordinarily strong community of leaders for the broader church.

Calvin's environment was a time and place in which many people believed that the way a community functioned reflected much of the quality of the faith of its citizens. Geneva carried out what other communities wanted to do but did not have the leadership, in church or in state, to accomplish. And, we must add, only during the last years of John Calvin's life did the city government and the church work in close harmony.

Many of Calvin's proposals for discipline either never received approval from the city or simply failed. One example was his plan to turn taverns into cafes with a Bible in each establishment, available for consultation during discussions among the customers. For quite a few pious Genevans this arrangement was just too much. The Bibles were eventually removed, and the more traditional facilities and refreshments returned.

The discipline the ministers wanted came only after years of political turmoil, with vigorous opposition from various factions within the city. Indeed, only the addition of hundreds of French religious refugees to the rolls of voters led the secular government to agree to enforce the moral laws the church wanted. Geneva never was a theocracy—a city governed by the church. However, a certain unanimity of purpose and direction often existed between the civil and the religious authorities.

Educational Reform

A significant accomplishment in the Genevan Reformation was the establishment of an educational system that, like Strasbourg, provided for education of all citizens, adults as well as children. The ministerial office of teacher provided the leadership for the entire structure.

The Genevan academy, the capstone of the program, was approved only late in Calvin's life and eventually became the University of Geneva. The academy provided not only a solid liberal arts education for the citizens of Geneva but also became a center for the training of ministers and laypeople who would provide leadership for the Reformation. The Genevan academy became a kind of mission school for Calvinism, and its success and influence is evident in the spread of Calvinism throughout much of Europe and later to the New World.

Protestant Unity in Switzerland

One of Calvin's major concerns was to bring about unity among the Protestants at least within Switzerland, which Geneva began to regard as a natural ally. One problem was that the chief centers of Reformation within Switzerland were Zurich and Bern. Zurich was under the leadership of Heinrich Bullinger, Zwingli's successor. Bullinger felt the need to protect both the reforms of Zwingli and Zwingli's place as founder and undisputed leader of the Swiss Reformation. To negotiate on points of difference with Geneva and to accept compromise on any issue would have been quite difficult for Bullinger and Zurich.

The problems Calvin encountered in dealing with Bern were based on Bern's position of greater political power than Geneva had, and Geneva's newfound political freedom was due in large measure to Bern's support. Bern, therefore, would not take direction from Geneva. However, Bern had no theological or pastoral leaders of Calvin's caliber.

The issues the Swiss theologians argued about were mostly minor, with the exception of the question of the Lord's Supper. The Zwinglian position on the nature of Christ's presence in the Lord's Supper emphasized a spiritual symbolism. Conflict with Luther had caused the Zwinglians to react with much stronger language about symbolic presence than was necessary. Calvin stood somewhere between the more extreme Zwinglian position and that of Luther. Closely following Martin Bucer's ideas, Calvin asserted that in faith and by the power of the Holy Spirit, the faithful believer receives along with the physical signs of bread and wine, the spiritual, real presence of Christ. As the body receives food for its sustenance, Christ's spirit nourishes the soul.

A series of debates, published arguments on both sides, and occasional challenges to Lutheran views pushed the discussion along throughout the 1540's. With skill and a good spirit on both sides, Calvin and Farel went to Zurich for a meeting in May 1549. In a matter of hours they reached an agreement. Summarized in the *Consensus Tigurinus*—the Zurich agreement—the Swiss Reformation was united under the joint leadership of Calvin and Bullinger.

The Servetus Affair

One of the most notorious events of the Reformation period was the trial and execution of Michael Servetus in Geneva. Servetus was a brilliant physician and theologian (as a medical scholar, he apparently discovered the principle of the pulmonary circulation of blood a century before it was generally accepted). He was also a radical thinker; and in a day that considered innovation to be wrongheaded at least, if not sinful and dangerous, Servetus dared to argue against the traditional doctrine of the Trinity.

Servetus lived and practiced medicine under assumed names, frequently changing his location. But in 1553, someone discovered Servetus's identity while he was serving as the personal physician of the archbishop of Vienne, in southeastern France. The Inquisition arrested and interrogated Servetus. Before the authorities brought him to trial, he escaped from prison. The Roman Catholic leaders therefore tried him in absentia and condemned him to be burned alive.

Servetus made the mistake of stopping over in Geneva, apparently so he could challenge Calvin. He attended services at Saint Peter's, where Calvin was preaching. Servetus was recognized, imprisoned, and tried for heresy. He gladly defended his views, thus confessing a kind of heresy that in the sixteenth century could only result in his death. He was again sentenced to be burned alive. Calvin vigorously opposed the form of execution (although he supported the death sentence itself), and pleaded for beheading instead so that Servetus would not suffer. The magistrates refused, and Servetus was burned at the stake. Protestants and Roman Catholics from all over Europe wrote letters of commendation and support for this action.

The issue was more than just another instance of grossly inhumane treatment of an individual and his ideas, though it was certainly that. The Servetus affair was also an important moment in terms of the Genevan Reformation and in terms of Calvin's stature as a leader of Protestantism. Calvin's opponents in Geneva decided to oppose Calvin on the matter of Servetus. But when they defended Servetus and lost, they gave up any remaining vestige of political power. Calvin's position reached its high point for the remaining eleven years of his life.

Geneva and Refugees

The location of Geneva at the headwaters of the Rhone River gave French Protestants a haven against persecution. During the reign of Mary Tudor of England (1553–1558), many English Protestants also found their way to Geneva. Refugees strained the resources of the Genevans. The deacons of the church were assigned the task of finding places for them to stay and making sure they had the basic necessities.

In addition to protection and shelter, Geneva offered educational opportunities. These Protestants who had already suffered much for their faith studied with Calvin and his coworkers. Many of these refugees eventually returned to their homelands and carried with them the structure, order, and zeal of Calvinist Protestantism. Printing presses in Geneva were put to work publishing Protestant books and pamphlets in various languages. The discipline of civic life in Geneva encouraged a personal discipline that worked itself out in lives of service.

Providing for refugees was only one part of the deacons' work. With the closing of monasteries, Protestants soon discovered that most of the social services that the monks and nuns had provided had to be made available some other way. Orphans, older adults, the poor, the sick, and people with handicapping conditions all had needs to be met.

Other Protestant cities and territories were experiencing much the same phenomenon. But Geneva, under Calvin's careful organizational plan, was able to respond to the social crisis more effectively than most other Protestant communities. For Calvin's Geneva the issue was not merely a matter of taking care of problems; it was an issue of ministry, of serving God's people, of being ministers.

The key to the brilliance of Calvin's Reformation was its logic, clarity, organization, and integration of the lived experience of ministry and worship with the theological principles on which faith was based. When we turn to Calvin's theology, we can gain a better understanding of the power of his movement.

---

[1] Quoted in *John Calvin: The Organizer of Reformed Protestantism 1509–1564*, by Williston Walker (Schocken Books, 1969); page 234.

4

Calvin as a Christian Theologian

Calvin was a much more systematic thinker than either Martin Luther or Ulrich Zwingli. Calvin's training in law, with its rigorous system of logic, can be seen in all that he wrote. Calvin's works on the Bible and on theology provided a body of literature that has shaped the minds and perspectives of generation after generation of Christian ministers and laypeople.

The *Institutes*

One of Calvin's most widely read books is the *Institutes of the Christian Religion*. The first edition was published in Basel in 1536, shortly before Calvin's initial stay in Geneva. This work announced to the world that a new force was present in the church in the person of a twenty-seven-year-old French lawyer and Protestant.

The *Institutes* would see several revisions over the years, up until the very end of Calvin's life. Calvin wrote the *Institutes* in Latin, but he prepared French translations of each major revision. The second edition of 1539 was twice as large as the first edition, and the last edition was twice as large again. The later editions were completely reorganized; but, for the most part, the revisions were a matter of "spelling out," making fuller and clearer what had been present from the beginning. Throughout this period Calvin was also engaged in writing commentaries on most of the books of the Bible, and each edition of the *Institutes of the Christian Religion* reveals additional references to and study of Scripture.

The Bible

Calvin's theology is firmly based on the Bible. Calvin believed that the Bible is God's Word made known, just as Jesus Christ is the Word made flesh. Calvin (and others of his era) did not address the questions of inerrancy or infallibility that people in the twentieth century often ask. Calvin assumed that the Bible is God's message and that in all matters relative to salvation Scripture represents perfect truth.

Calvin argued for a straightforward, literal interpretation of Scripture. He acknowledged that while the Holy Spirit guided the writers of the Bible, the writers were themselves individual human beings with personal histories. He felt that their view of realilty was shaped by conditions of time and place, history and language. These factors mean that the interpreters of Scripture have to proceed carefully and prudently. But they can always be confident that the truth can be known.

Thus, all theology, all matters of faith and practice that are of any significance, can be found in the Bible. And all Christian life and thought is to be judged by the standard of the Bible.

Because of the significance of the Bible for Calvin and for all early Protestants, Calvin argued for educational structures that would provide training in the biblical languages. John Calvin wanted this training not only for prospective pastors but also for those laypeople who would be leaders of their communities.

The Church and Its Ministry

The ultimate shape and structure of the *Institutes* followed the outline of the classic statements of the early church, the Nicene Creed and the Apostles' Creed. In this way Calvin was making an important statement about the nature of the Reformation. According to Calvin, the Reformation had to do with the universal church. The Protestant movement was not a break with the true church but was the heart and soul of the church as established by Jesus and led by Peter and Paul and Augustine and the other faithful Christians of the ages. And, most important, Calvin believed that the church exists wherever the Word is preached and the sacraments are administered, regardless of the name of the group.

However, Calvin also believed that the Church of Rome had largely departed from the path of the true church and that the genuine church existed among the newly reformed churches. Nevertheless, Calvin thought that the unity of the church, the unity of Christ, is found in the faithful observance of the people gathered, not in the names those people have.

According to Calvin, the ministry of the church goes far beyond the various tasks assigned to the offices of pastor, teacher, elder, and deacon. The minister is an agent and ambassador for the gospel of Jesus Christ. The pastor and teacher have special responsibility as interpreters and proclaimers of the Word (Christ) through exposition of the Word (Scripture).

The pastor and the elder have the heavy burden of discipline in the church, that is, the maintenance of proper morals and doctrine. Calvin believed that without careful attention to discipline, the church could not survive. He said, "As the saving doctrine of Christ is the soul of the church, so does discipline serve as its sinews, through which the members of the body hold together, each in its own place."[1] One crucial characteristic of the church was that it exercise discipline according to the teachings of Scripture, particularly the New Testament.

God

Scripture gives light to the church, and the church makes witness to the Word. But what is the character of the God who speaks to people through Scripture and through the church? According to Calvin, one of the most fundamental concepts for Christians to understand is that God is God. God is the ruler, the sovereign of all that is, of all that may be, and of all that will be. All that is good comes from the loving kindness of God. All that is bad or evil comes from resistance to God and rebellion against God.

Sin

Human beings, although God created them, are not themselves God. When they disobey God, they break faith with God; and this disobedience is called sin. God commands human beings to be obedient. So, as soon as they sin, even just a little, they have separated themselves from the glory and majesty of God. No act by the individual or by the community can restore sinners to God's grace. Any good thing they do is simply doing that which they are always expected to do.

Human sin, therefore, has created a chasm between God and people, a chasm that only God can bridge. And God, acting out of love and compassion and forgiveness, chose to build such a bridge, to reach out to humankind.

God's Work in Christ

This wonderful bridge is grace. Grace is a gift that no one can earn. God's grace has made it possible for humankind to be returned to God. The instrument of God's grace is Jesus, his life and, more important, his death on a cross. Because Jesus lived a life without blemish, a life without sin, he did not need to pay the penalty for sin: death. But Jesus did just that. Jesus took on the sins of humankind even though he had none of his own. Having thus paid the price of death, Jesus Christ is able to offer life to sinful humankind.

Because of the sacrifice of Jesus, God counts Jesus Christ's goodness instead of human sinfulness. Through faith people receive this grace that saves. Faith, then, is the key to the human experience of salvation.

Faith

According to Calvin, faith is trusting God, relying on God to be true to the promises made through Jesus. Faith is that which believes that humankind will receive the benefits of Christ Jesus' sacrifice. Faith is having now in hope what we will one day have in fullness. Faith is both the knowledge of what God has done and confidence that God is trustworthy.

Salvation

Calvin, like Luther, believed that for a person to try to earn or buy God's favor was to belittle the price Jesus paid on Golgotha. Calvin and Luther believed that only by putting all faith in God, by putting all trust in God's gracious gift of salvation, could a person have any sense of confidence. Only by relying solely on God could individuals be relieved of the agony of wondering if they had done enough to satisfy a righteous God.

Predestination

We need to look at Calvin's famous teachings on predestination in this context. Calvin believed that because only God acting through Jesus Christ can bring salvation to sinful humankind, God must be the author of that salvation. Since some people clearly refused to have faith and some people made so little effort to try to live in light of God's love, Calvin thought that the offer of salvation must have been withheld from some human beings.

Since everyone, every single person, deserves damnation because of the sin in which all persons participate, any action by God to save even one person is a deed of wondrously undeserved grace. For many people to receive the gift of salvation simply adds to the signs of God's extraordinary love. Those persons who are hardened by their sin and refuse to turn to God are those who have been condemned, justly in Calvin's view, for their sin.

Thus, all people who truly struggle to live a life of faithful obedience, even if they sometimes stumble, can be assured that God has called them to salvation. In this way Christians can escape the anxiety and fear that would come from trying to save themselves. Predestination becomes an instrument of pastoral care, a doctrine of loving concern arising out of a loving God and proclaimed by a servant church.

Calvin confronted all the standard challenges to predestination in his own lifetime. He answered many of these challenges before anyone raised them. He showed, he believed, that most opposition to predestination was based either on an understanding of God that would greatly limit God's power or on an understanding of salvation that would put a great burden on the shoulders of the believer. Calvin was adamant in his position. He firmly believed that predestination is the action of a loving God giving gifts where none are due, even as Jesus the Son was sent into a world that did not deserve him.

Ironically, Calvin has come down through history as the great advocate of predestination, even though Luther and Zwingli were equally strong in their belief in the concept. And none of these reformers spent as much time and energy on predestination as their descendants have.

Law

If sin is rebellion against God, the main expression of sin is to be found in disobedience to God's law. God's law is found in the Old Testament. The Old

Testament contains several layers of law, including laws limited to the ancient Hebrew people, laws that applied to particular places and times, and laws that had universal significance.

The laws of universal application are summarized in the ancient statement, "Hear, O Israel: the LORD our God is one LORD" (Deuteronomy 6:4). This summary is elaborated in various ways in the Bible. Jesus confirmed this law in a passage in which the love of neighbor as self is upheld as a corollary to loving God (Mark 12:28-34). For Calvin, the Ten Commandments form the heart of the law, the great statement of what God would have us do to live as God's own people. Calvin upheld the Ten Commandments not only as the center of the law but also as a significant part of worship to be heard, chanted, sung, preached, and lived.

Like Luther, Calvin believed that the law provides the standard of godliness that convicts humankind of sin. Over against the law human society and individual lives are found wanting. The law is a mirror in which the glory of God is contrasted with the sinfulness of humankind. The law thus upholds the righteousness of God.

The law also provides the rulers of the earth with a standard by which to maintain order. Only when people obey the secular powers can the gospel be preached.

For Calvin, however, the law had a third use. Calvin taught that the law is also a guide for Christians, individually and in community, to live the life that God would have us live. The first two uses of the law are largely negative and restraining in character, but the third use of the law is a positive statement and can be used for imaginative creation of a new world. This more positive understanding of the law apparently gave Calvinistic Protestants a level of zeal and enthusiasm that led them to be pioneers for the Christian community (pioneers in the literal sense in the New World, pioneers in a more figurative sense in the Old World). They tried to restructure the ways in which Christians might live together in cities and in nations.

Sacraments

While God offers salvation freely through grace by faith, God also knows the limitations of human beings. Calvin taught that because we are creatures, physical beings often limited by our very flesh, God gives signs and symbols of the divine love. These signs and symbols are called sacraments.

Calvin accepted Martin Luther's limiting of sacraments to baptism and the Lord's Supper. He agreed that only those acts that Jesus Christ clearly commanded and ordained should be considered sacraments. According to Calvin, the wonder of the sacraments is to be found in the use of physical matter (things of the earth such as water, bread, and wine) as vehicles for the most wondrous of all spiritual gifts, God's loving grace.

The sacraments are, therefore, rooted in creation yet convey the message of the Creator. They point to what God has done in Jesus Christ. In the water of baptism sins are washed away, a sign of Jesus cleaning up a corrupted world by his sacrifice of himself. The water of baptism is a symbol of God's accepting us as if we were without sin.

The breaking of bread and the pouring of wine symbolize the breaking of the body of Jesus and the spilling of his blood, even as God's love poured out is seen in the loaf and in the cup. The Lord's Supper renews again and again the experience of forgiveness first known in the waters of baptism.

Both sacraments point to the significance of the Christian community. Baptism inducts the new Christian into the community of believers. The Lord's Supper is the feast of the community, the church.

The sacraments became for Calvin another expression of the character of God's love for creation. Not only does God make use of the things of creation to help us perceive God's loving gifts. Through the natural acts of washing and eating and drinking, the human soul is nourished by spiritual gifts of grace. "When bread is given as a symbol of Christ's body, we must at once grasp this comparison: as bread nourishes, sustains, and keeps the life of our body, so Christ's body is the only food to invigorate and enliven our soul."[2]

The key to a spiritual reception of Christ is faith. Without faith, no spiritual benefit exists. When the body feeds on bread and wine *in faith*, the human spirit receives the very body and blood of Jesus Christ as a spiritual gift.

In sum, the sacraments, like Scripture, have value and meaning so long as they hold forth Christ.

The Bible Teacher

In addition to the *Institutes* and other theological treatises, Calvin delivered sermons, lectured on Scripture, and wrote commentaries on almost all the books of the Bible.

The result of all this time and attention Calvin gave to Scripture was that Calvin's profound knowledge of Scripture shaped everything he did. His writings on the Bible were particularly clear and precise, and they encouraged the reader to go directly to the Bible to read and study and meditate.

Calvin's preaching schedule was quite heavy. He preached on the New Testament on Sundays, sometimes on the Psalms on Sunday afternoons, and on the Old Testament through the week. For several years he preached each day of the week (every other week) as well as twice on Sunday. One consequence of this schedule was that Calvin did little direct preparation for preaching and allowed his writing of Bible commentaries to serve as preparation. He would take his Greek New Testament or Hebrew Old Testament into the pulpit and read, translating by sight, the portion assigned for the day (usually picking up from where he left off the last time). Then he commented on the passage. Fortunately, from 1549 on, an official note taker kept a verbatim record of all Calvin's sermons, using a kind of shorthand.

Calvin's Death

In February 1564, Calvin's lifelong bouts with various illnesses began to bring his life to a close. He preached for the last time on February 6. He tried to continue to work at home, dictating letters and revisions of various works. In April he made out his will. Calvin had little to give to his heirs. He had intentionally never made much money and always gave away substantial portions of what he had.

The members of the Geneva City Council came to see Calvin. He encouraged them to trust God and to look for leadership by the Holy Spirit. He gave a long, rambling statement, in part reflecting on his career, to the ministers when they gathered. He named Theodore Beza, the young professor of theology in the academy, to be his successor. Old William Farel made a final visit. Two weeks later, on May 27, 1564, Calvin died. He was buried in the paupers' cemetery in an unmarked, common grave. Calvin had requested this simple burial so that no one would make a shrine of his final resting place.

With Calvin's death the Reformation entered a new phase. Virtually all the first wave of Reformation leaders were gone. Protestantism represented not only a division of the church but a shattering of the church. Yet, the Reformation continued. While Lutheranism largely consolidated its territorial gains during the second half of the sixteenth century, Calvinism continued to expand and grow throughout Europe. In England the movement for reform of the church was still young and was not yet moving in a clear direction. To this expansion of the Reformation we will turn in the next chapters.

---

[1]From *Calvin: Institutes of the Christian Religion*, edited by John T. McNeill (The Westminster Press, 1960); Book IV, Chapter 12:1.

[2]From *Calvin: Institutes of the Christian Religion*; Book IV, Chapter 17:3.

5

The Spread of the Reformation on the European Continent

Traces of the Reformation could be found throughout much of Europe within a few years after Luther wrote his "Ninety-five Theses." Lutheranism moved from eastern and northern Germany to Scandinavia and Eastern Europe and to the West. The movement even reached the Netherlands, Great Britain, and France.

However, a major presence of Protestantism in many of these lands had to await the arrival of Calvinist Protestants. In some countries, such as France, the success (albeit a short-lived and limited success) of Protestantism was due to the work of the followers of Calvin.

Calvinism, then, seemed to travel better than Luther's movement. Calvinism was more successful as an international evangelistic effort than was Lutheranism. The reasons are not entirely clear. Many partisans are quick to point out the advantages and disadvantages of each perspective.

However, we can make at least these "neutral" observations. Calvin's Reformation, Calvinism, was far less tied to the power and vigor of one particular charismatic personality than was the case with Lutheranism. Furthermore, after John Calvin's death the movement still had a few clearly recognizable leaders whom people could turn to for guidance. The most significant of these leaders was Theodore Beza. The Lutherans had no such unifying force and spent much more energy dealing with internal struggles than did the Calvinists during this period of time. (The Calvinists would face a similar conflict early in the next century, but by that time they were already well established).

The structure of the church under Calvin's design made it adaptable to difficult and even to hostile conditions. The church did not need support by the secular government. The church and its ministry were self-regulating and capable of independent existence. Luther's design for the structure of the church tended to be much more closely tied to the state. Where the state was not an advocate of the church, Lutheranism generally did not do well, at least not in the sixteenth century.

Also, the Calvinist movement quickly found itself in positions of strength in different national and language settings, including the Swiss German of Zurich, Bern, and Basel; the independent and French Swiss areas of Geneva and Lausanne; and in various locations in France. Supporters of Calvinist—that is, Reformed—Protestantism were also active in southern Germany and in some of the cities along the Rhine Valley. Calvinists were even present in Flemish and in Dutch-speaking areas of the Netherlands. Calvinism also had support in England.

These various places of support and the variety of languages involved meant that Calvinism and Calvinist leaders understood themselves to be part of a movement that went far beyond their own narrow interests. In spite of the rising nationalism that was an important part of this period in history, Calvinism took on an international character that helped the leading Reformed ministers and laypeople think about the needs and concerns of fellow Protestants in other lands.

Calvinism in Germany

People in southern Germany held Reformed views quite early due to proximity to Zwingli's Zurich. Even before Zwingli's death the cities of this region began to rely on the leadership of Martin Bucer of Strasbourg. He functioned as a kind of missionary bishop throughout the territory. With his influence the southern Germans very easily received Calvin's ideas and suggestions quite positively. While they were never blindly Calvinistic, the southern Germans did represent yet another area of expansion for Reformed Protestantism.

Luther died in 1546. The next year the Schmalkaldic Wars began with an initial victory for the Roman Catholic forces of Charles V over the Protestants. In 1555, the wars had ended on a note of Protestant triumph. The weary and aging emperor was willing to settle his German affairs. The resulting peace treaty gave official status to Lutherans and to Roman Catholics but none to other Protestants.

Calvin's Reformed movement seemed to be in great difficulty in Germany. Even Strasbourg, home of Martin Bucer, had become strongly Lutheran after Bucer and the other Reformed pastors had been forced to flee for their lives during the wars.

However, about the time of Calvin's death, the Reformed cause began to find new life in Germany, particularly in the Palatinate, a region with fabled Heidelberg at its very center. In the University of Heidelberg, where Calvinism was allowed to coexist with Lutheranism, a narrowly partisan Lutheran professor named Tilemann Hesshus made a strong verbal attack on all divergence from Luther's views. He was especially harsh on the Calvinism of some persons in the university. Hesshus's barrage backfired. People thought his negative spirit was uncharitable and bigoted. The prince of the Palatinate, Elector Frederick III, decided to become a supporter of Calvinism. Through his efforts Heidelberg became not only a place where Calvinist theology was welcome but also became almost another Geneva, another training center for Calvinist militants.

Frederick succeeded in bringing two young, brilliant Reformed theologians to Heidelberg to teach and preach. Zacharias Ursinus and Caspar Olevianus first prepared a catechism for the education of children into the faith. This Heidelberg Catechism, published in 1563, became a classic summary statement of Calvinist theology. It was soon translated into Dutch for use in the churches of the Netherlands.

Unlike most catechisms this work used the personal language of "me" and "my" and made frequent references to God as "my God" and "my Father." Designed for the education of children, the Heidelberg Cathechism was easily adaptable as a guide to private devotions and worship in family settings.

Frederick also directed the establishment of a form of worship that was largely dependent on Calvin and Bucer. The churches in the Palatinate were restructured according to Reformed principles.

When Frederick died in 1576, his son succeeded him. Louis VI was as strongly Lutheran as his father had been Calvinist. Some six hundred Calvinist preachers and professors were sent into exile. The unintended result was to send six hundred missionaries for Calvinism throughout Germany. When Louis VI died after only seven years of rule, the Palatinate returned to the Calvinist ranks; and Calvinism had made inroads in many communities and principalities in Germany.

Bohemia and Moravia

In Bohemia and in Moravia (both in what is now Czechoslovakia), Protestantism had experienced a head start during the early fifteenth century. The followers of pre-Protestant reformer John Huss had established their own church only to divide into the Utraquists and the Unity of the Brethren. They responded positively to the Lutheran Reformation and began a move to unite with the Lutherans in the

1540's. However, many of the nobles sent their youth to Geneva and Zurich and Strasbourg to study. By 1555, a number of the Brethren had become Calvinists.

After a century and a half of religious struggle, the Bohemians and Moravians agreed to work together. They decided to allow Lutherans and Calvinists to coexist so as to put up a common front against Roman Catholic Counter Reformation efforts. The Bohemians flourished until 1618 and the outbreak of the Thirty Years' War, a devastating war between Protestants and Roman Catholics that began in Prague, the capital of Bohemia.

The Moravian branch of the church also suffered persecution but finally found peace and an opportunity to rebuild under the protection of Count von Zinzendorf in the early eighteenth century. The Moravians had a profound influence on John Wesley, the founder of Methodism.

France

France had been an early center of the Renaissance. As the life of Calvin has revealed, people in France knew and advocated Luther's views soon after the beginning of the Reformation. But Lutheranism had only modest success. The Protestant cause in France was scattered, mostly sporadic and unfocused, until the Reformed Protestants began to exercise some leadership there.

One of the first of the Reformed theologians to work for the cause in France was William Farel. He preached in the area of Montbeliard as early as the 1520's. He served in the Swiss regions for a number of years and returned to France in 1542 as a minister in Lorraine. He experienced severe persecution, was trapped in a castle under siege by Roman Catholic troops, and escaped to Switzerland with a new reputation for bravery and courage.

During the 1550's, a number of prominent French noble families became Protestants. Among these people was Jeanne d'Albret, the daughter of Marguerite d'Angouleme. Marguerite, sister of King Francis I, had protected Calvin some years earlier. Jeanne was not only the daughter of a powerful woman, she would also be the mother of a future king of France, Henry IV.

The French Protestants, called Huguenots (scholars do not agree on the origin of the word), were persecuted under King Henry II (he ruled during the years 1547–1559). Many of the Huguenots fled for periods of time to Geneva. Under Francis I the Protestants had experienced occasional fierce persecution, but under Henry II the policy was more consistent. His goal was their extermination.

Henry established new court procedures so that Protestants could be convicted more easily. Execution was by burning at the stake. Because a number of people became converts as a result of the courageous statements Huguenots made as they were being burned at the stake, the authorities instituted a policy of cutting out the tongues of those to be burned.

The Protestants who reached Geneva received shelter and protection as well as instruction in the faith. They then returned to France as determined advocates of Protestantism. They often carried back with them books and pamphlets intended to win over still more French citizens to the Protestant faith.

The nobles who were moving into the Protestant ranks were generally members of the families that were in opposition to the most rigorous defenders of Roman Catholicism. When Henry II died in 1559, he left behind three very young sons. Each of them would be king, and each of them would be a very weak ruler. The combination of religious and political unrest led to a series of conflicts that resulted in bloodshed.

In March 1562, a group of Protestants were worshiping in a barn near Vassy. Soldiers surrounded the barn and set it on fire. As the Protestants tried to escape the flames, the soldiers shot them. The Protestants who remained behind burned to death.

This event began a series of wars that would last until 1598. Called the Wars of Religion, and religion was certainly an issue, the conflict was even more a civil war by which various factions of the French nobility and society sought power and security.

Each side was guilty of moral outrage. Each side participated in slaughter. However, none of the violent incidents equalled that of Saint Bartholomew's Day, August 23–24, 1572, when the authorities attempted to destroy Protestantism in France. In a matter of just a few weeks, some twenty thousand Protestants were murdered. Several thousand were killed in Paris. The Seine River seemed to overflow with bodies. The result was to intensify the Protestant resistance and also to bring foreign support for the Protestants from all sides.

In Geneva, gunpowder manufacturing became an important industry along with printing. Refugees carried bags of gunpowder along with Protestant tracts as they traveled along mountain paths back to France.

The Wars of Religion concluded with Protestant Henry of Navarre becoming King Henry IV of France, after he returned to the Roman Catholic Church. Henry issued the Edict of Nantes which theoretically gave Protestantism in France a legal basis and protection from persecution.

The Protestant church in France became a significant minority church. Somewhere between one tenth and one third of the population were members. The lower number is probably closer to the mark. In some areas and in some cities, Protestants represented a significant presence. In other areas few supporters of Protestantism were active.

However, because its fight for survival had been waged through war and political conflict, the Protestant cause in France was vulnerable. Under steady royal pressure the Huguenots were increasingly isolated in the seventeenth century. King Louis XIV was able to revoke the Edict of Nantes in 1685, and Protestants had to flee "underground" or into exile. At significant cost in human talent, France largely eliminated the Protestant presence.

The Netherlands

If the French Protestants ultimately lost the struggle for the right to exist, Dutch Protestants tell a different story, even though they shared some similarities with the French.

The Netherlands were under the personal control of the Hapsburg family. When the Reformation erupted, Charles V, unable to impose his will on the Holy Roman Empire, largely suppressed any inclination toward Protestantism in the Low Countries. Under that general name of *Netherlands,* or *Low Countries,* was included the modern-day Netherlands (the Dutch nation, of which Holland is the largest state), Belgium, Luxembourg, and a section of what is now northern France.

While the Protestant gains in the Netherlands were quite modest while Charles ruled, the Protestant cause began to move forward after his resignation and death. Under Charles's son, Philip II (of Spain), a very different situation existed. Charles had been a strict ruler, but he was born and raised in the Low Countries. People considered him to be a legitimate ruler. Philip, however, was Spanish by upbringing, by language, and by nature. People thought of him as an absentee landlord, and any conflict with his representatives took on the added factor of "foreign" interference.

Philip used Spanish soldiers to keep order in the Low Countries. He was quick to use force to root out any possible heresy, any sign of the Protestant menace. The reaction of the Dutch was to oppose what they regarded as a loss of ancient liberties. Time and again the authorities treated political resistance to Philip's policies as a form of advocacy of Protestantism, and Protestantism was indeed beginning to infiltrate all levels of society. The Protestants had no reason to be supportive of the vigorously anti-Protestant Philip, and they had every reason to give aid to the movement for Dutch independence.

One of the most prominent of the Dutch resisters

was William, Prince of Orange. He came to be known as William the Silent. William became the primary leader of the Protestant and independence cause. The Protestant side of the conflict came into the open only a number of years after the war for independence was underway, though William's marriage to a German Protestant was certainly an indication of his preferences.

The Protestant cause was advanced after the arrival in 1561 of Guy de Bres, who had grown up in Geneva. He prepared a Calvinist confession of faith, called the Belgic Confession. Dutch Calvinists accepted it in 1566 at a meeting in Antwerp.

The Reformation had its first success in the southern, French-speaking areas of the Low Countries. However, the spread of Calvinism to the northern, Dutch-speaking provinces was rapid, much more thorough, and permanent.

Conflict between the Netherlanders and Philip II grew each time he demanded higher taxes and each time he called for suppression of Protestantism. Philip sent heavy-handed military leaders to enforce his will. As a result, the members of the opposition united. Sporadic violence occurred from 1566 onwards. Full-fledged war began in 1567. Thousands of Protestants were executed. This series of events resulted in the virtual uniting of the independence movement with Protestantism.

The southern provinces gradually withdrew from the militantly Calvinist northern provinces. One result was that Protestantism eventually died out in the French-speaking area. After decades of war and international intrigue, the northern provinces were essentially recognized as a sovereign nation in 1609. As a nation forged in war, shaped and supported by the Reformed churches of the region, the Netherlands became a place of vigorous Calvinism.

The Netherlands soon became a major world economic power. Through the colonizing efforts of seventeenth-century Dutch merchants, the Protestant message was carried to far parts of the world, from

Borneo to Johannesburg to Manhattan. (The Dutch Calvinists were the people who bought Manhattan Island from the Native Americans for, according to legend, beads worth twenty-four dollars.)

Protestantism and Revolution

One result of years of warfare and struggle for survival by Calvin's followers was the development of a new idea of government. Calvin was reluctant to say anything favorable about revolution. However, the horrors of state-sponsored repression finally led him to admit that when a ruler failed to carry out the responsibilities of office (especially if the ruler became a tyrant), other governmental officers might appropriately take over the office of the ruler.

From this point it was a short distance to argue for the legitimacy of armed rebellion against tyrants; and then, ultimately, it was possible to argue for representative government. Another century would pass before the basic ideas were fully formulated and stated and another century again before such values were finally put into action in the American Revolution. However, the origins of these values, at least in part, are to be found in the efforts of Protestants, particularly Calvinist Protestants, to live their faith without persecution. From a barn in Vassy, France, to the dikes around Amsterdam, to the streets of Prague, the Reformation became a revolution in the way people understood themselves as a community.

6

A New Protestantism: Calvin Refined

The English Reformation has a history that is in many ways quite different from what happened on the European continent. The story was much more closely tied to kings and queens and the legislature than was the case on the Continent.

Forerunners of the Reformation were active in England. In the fourteenth century an Oxford professor named John Wyclif challenged the wealth and privileges of the church in his day. (See *Early Reformers: Winds of Change* in this series for more information about Wyclif.) He began a translation of the Bible into English that became the first complete English Bible. His followers were ridiculed and called Lollards (perhaps mimicking the many uneducated speakers among them). During the fifteenth century just to be a Lollard was a crime punishable by death.

As some preparation of the English soil took place as a result of the work of the Lollards, so did much nurturing occur through the activities of English Renaissance humanists. Thomas More and John Colet were both intimate friends of Erasmus. A number of other English humanists were also his friends. Erasmus spent many happy days in England. In the universities and in the courts of nobles, even in some of the churches, humanists were at work studying Scripture and pondering Paul. These people were becoming increasingly critical of the quality of the work the church was performing.

Henry VIII and Protestantism

Henry VIII was never supposed to have been king. Arthur, his brother, was the heir apparent. A political marriage was arranged for Arthur with Catherine of Aragon, a Spanish princess. But Arthur died young, so the throne came to Henry VIII when his father died. Henry's father, Henry VII, had become king as a result of the bloody civil war known as the War of the Roses. Vast slaughter of the young noblemen of England during that war led every thinking English citizen to want to avoid another civil war at all costs.

So, to maintain continuity and to build stronger foreign relationships, Henry VIII married his brother's widow. Henry and Catherine had only one child who survived, a daughter named Mary.

Henry had originally been educated for a career in the church. He had studied the rudiments of theology and was a bright student. He had a colossal ego; and when Luther attacked the Roman Catholic doctrine of the sacraments, Henry wrote (he may have received assistance from others) a little book titled *The Defense of the Seven Sacraments*. For this support of the Roman Catholic position, the pope awarded Henry the title "Defender of the Faith."

Henry's personal faith was deeply rooted in the traditions of the medieval church, and he defended Roman Catholicism vigorously. But an extremely complicated situation soon affected his attitude toward the church.

Henry became concerned that he and Catherine had not had a son. He seems to have been genuinely fearful that he had broken one of God's laws by marrying his brother's widow, despite the fact that the pope had given him special permission to do so. Leviticus 18:16a says, "You shall not uncover the

55

nakedness of your brother's wife." Some people interpreted this statement as not only prohibiting adultery with a sister-in-law but also as prohibiting a man from marrying his brother's widow. Henry was fearful that the several miscarriages and stillbirths indicated God's displeasure with him. In addition, the history of women on the throne in England was short and ugly. So, the prospects for Mary's potential rule were not encouraging.

Henry's growing infatuation with a young woman of the court, Anne Boleyn, complicated the situation further. Henry had many mistresses and casual affairs, and Anne's sister had been one of his favorite consorts. Anne refused to accept Henry's advances unless he agreed to make her queen.

Henry ordered Cardinal Wolsey, who served as the pope's representative in England, to obtain permission from the Holy See to divorce Catherine. The public reason was the lack of a male heir, seen as a punishment for Henry's marriage to his brother's widow.

At first Henry thought that this process would be relatively simple. A certain amount of time would be required for the bureaucratic procedures, and that could be shortened with bribes in the right places. But a complication developed.

About this time, 1527, the pope was captured in a war with the Holy Roman Emperor, Charles V. The pope had been in alliance with France against the Empire. Charles V was the nephew of Catherine of Aragon; and she had let him know that she would be deeply disgraced by a divorce, even by an annulment. Once released from captivity, the pope was still in a position where Charles could move against him at will. The "simple process" was not only no longer simple, it was impossible.

Henry was furious. His desire for Anne Boleyn grew with her continued refusals. His fear of what would happen to England if he did not have a male heir ate away at him. Separating out all these motives is not easy, perhaps not even possible.

Henry hoped to avoid a complete break with Rome, but by early 1533 the circumstances warranted more drastic action. Anne was pregnant. With Thomas Cranmer as archbishop and with dire threats from Henry, the English church proclaimed Henry divorced from Catherine. Henry said that he and Anne had been married in January but that their public marriage could take place only after the conclusion of the divorce. In September, Anne gave birth. The child was a daughter. They named her Elizabeth.

A series of acts by Parliament slowly broke the ties with Rome. In 1534, the final steps were taken. No more money was to be sent to Rome. The Act of Succession made Elizabeth the heir apparent, and the Act of Supremacy made Henry the head of the Church of England. Several prominent people, including Sir Thomas More and Bishop John Fisher, were beheaded for their refusal to accept the changes.

Meanwhile, the reform, however modest, was underway. All monasteries were closed, and the crown confiscated their property. Henry used this wealth primarily to buy support and allegiance from certain nobles, from prominent farmers who wanted to move up the social and economic ladder, and from merchants. Only limited sums were used to carry on the work of the monasteries in providing schools and care for the poor, older adults, and the sick. A minor rebellion against the dissolution of the monasteries was put down easily and brutally.

Henry found himself the head of the church, a position he seemed to enjoy. However, he needed to make alliances with Protestants and thus make concessions to the Reformation in his own land. That idea did not appeal to Henry at all.

Nevertheless, changes were slowly made. In 1537, a new edition of the Bible was allowed to be published. The Protestant marginal notes disturbed Henry. He tried to suppress that edition while supporting a revision by Miles Coverdale. This work, called the Great Bible, appeared in 1540 and was placed in every church in England.

In response to Roman Catholic opposition to the changes in the church, Henry forced the church to accept the Ten Articles in 1536. While these articles were barely Protestant, they were more Protestant than Roman Catholic and moved the church a little more away from Rome and toward Wittenberg.

Just as Henry had reacted against Roman Catholic complaints, Henry reacted angrily to calls for more forthright reform. As a result, the Six Articles of 1539 upheld such doctrines as a traditional Roman Catholic understanding of the meaning of the Lord's Supper, forbade the laity to receive the cup, prohibited marriage of the clergy, and supported monastic vows (in the same year as the large monasteries were closed). The penalty for violation of these articles was at least imprisonment. A second infraction would result in certain death. The process of Protestantization slowed to a crawl.

Meanwhile, Anne had not been able to bear a male child; and Henry again felt the pangs of conscience. This time his conscience was aided by the appearance of young Jane Seymour in the court. Anne was charged with adultery, which for the wife of the king amounted to treason. She was convicted on fraudulent and torture-induced evidence. Anne died proclaiming her innocence, her loyalty to Henry, and her allegiance to the Protestant cause.

Henry married Jane Seymour in 1536. The next year she presented Henry with a male heir, Edward. But Jane died shortly after childbirth.

At this point foreign policy concerns interfered with Henry's selection of a mate. Thomas Cromwell (Henry's chief adviser) convinced Henry that England needed an alliance with some of the Protestant German states. So, Henry married by proxy a Protestant princess named Anne of Cleves. When the bride and groom finally had the opportunity to meet, each was distressed by the appearance of the other (court painters had supplied flattering portraits of the two).

Furthermore, by the time Anne arrived, the danger

of war with Charles V seemed to be far less a threat than Henry had originally thought. The marriage was annulled, to the great relief of both Anne and Henry. However, for Cromwell the issue was grave. He had recommended a strong Protestant foreign policy, he had helped arrange the marriage, and Henry was furious. The king sent Cromwell to the block. With a stroke of the headman's ax, Henry destroyed his most loyal subject.

Henry's last two marriages were of opposite sorts. First Henry married Catherine Howard, who actually did what Anne Boleyn had been accused of doing. Caught in adultery, Catherine was executed.

Henry then turned to a widow named Catherine Parr. She served him primarily as nurse in his last years and outlived Henry.

The Edwardian Reformation

Before Henry died, he made arrangements for a council of regents to rule in Edward's name until Edward reached adulthood. In 1547, Edward VI became king even though he was not quite ten years old.

Henry balanced his appointment of regents between Protestants and Roman Catholics, but surely he must have realized that the dominant figures were Protestant. Under their leadership England moved much more intentionally into the Protestant camp.

The regents directed Thomas Cranmer to prepare worship and administrative guidelines for a reformed church. The most important work to come during this period, and Cranmer's monument in history, was the *Book of Common Prayer*, a directory of worship with prescribed orders of worship and prayers.

The first edition was published in 1549. Martin Bucer, who had just arrived from Strasbourg as a refugee, was asked to prepare a critical response. He did, drawing on his own vast knowledge of worship and on the writings of Martin Luther, John Calvin, and Ulrich Zwingli. Many of Bucer's suggestions were incorporated in the second edition of the book.

The Reformation was proceeding rapidly throughout England under the direction of the government of the "boy king." But Edward was not well; he never had been. He died in 1553, and with only modest opposition his half sister Mary succeeded him.

The Marian Reaction

Mary was the daughter of Catherine of Aragon. Mary had been raised Roman Catholic, an outcast in her own country. She called Roman Catholics back from exile and began a re-Catholicization of England. Several hundred Protestant clergypersons and some prominent laypersons fled the country. These people were called the Marian exiles.

Those Protestants who could not run, or did not run, paid a price. About three hundred people were executed, mostly by burning. Among these persons was Thomas Cranmer. The bones of Martin Bucer were exhumed and burned. Mary received the name *Bloody Mary*.

The English people had initially received Mary well. Most of them agreed that she was the legitimate heir. But her harsh repression of Protestantism and her marriage to the Spanish prince (later king) Philip II cost her much English affection. The people shed few tears when she died in 1558.

The Elizabethan Settlement

The reign of Mary had allowed Roman Catholics to come out of hiding and to be forthright in the expression of their faith. But they soon had to worry again. Mary was followed on the throne by Elizabeth, the daughter of Henry VIII and Anne Boleyn.

Elizabeth found herself in a difficult situation. She found much meaning in worship that was Roman Catholic in style, but her base of power was in the ranks of Protestants. Mary Stuart, the queen of Scotland, claimed the English throne for herself.

Elizabeth's advisers believed Mary was conspiring with Roman Catholic France and English Roman Catholic noble families to overthrow Elizabeth.

When Elizabeth turned to the Protestants for support, she found that the very moderate Protestant direction of Cranmer's movement of reform was being challenged. The Protestants who had fled England during Mary's reign had lived in Zurich, in Geneva, and in Frankfort. They had been exposed to the much more radical ideas of Calvin and Zwingli and the Reformed brand of Protestantism.

These Marian exiles were calling for a more thorough Reformation, and that was something that Elizabeth clearly did not want. Elizabeth appointed Matthew Parker to be her archbishop of Canterbury. He was a more moderate Protestant, though very much influenced by Calvin. Under his leadership a new prayer book was issued, and a modest reform began.

Many Protestants responded by calling for a purification of the Church of England. As a result, they came to be known as *Puritans*. The people who supported Elizabeth's approach to the Reformation were called *Anglicans*. Like Elizabeth, they saw their movement to be somewhere between the Protestantism of the Continent and Roman Catholicism. They believed that they had the best of both traditions, with a theological emphasis on salvation by the grace of God but with forms and structures of worship based on ancient tradition.

The close identity of Anglicanism with some aspects of Roman Catholicism and the role of the monarch as supreme governor of the church (instead of Henry's language of "supreme head") meant that the Anglican church put more emphasis on ceremony and on formal vestments worn by the priests of the church than other branches of Protestantism did. These items thus became some of the major points of controversy between the Puritans and those who agreed with Elizabeth.

By the early 1580's, some of the Puritans wearied of

"purifying" the Anglican church and argued for separating themselves from it. They called for a separation of church and state and organized themselves into simple worshiping communities. They suffered much persecution.

Some of the Puritans emigrated to the more tolerant Netherlands. These people lived there in peace but began to worry about their children growing up more Dutch than English. In 1620, these religious pilgrims boarded a small ship named the *Mayflower* and sailed for a new land and new opportunities.

Others of the Separatists, some under the strong influence of Calvin's theology, took even more radical positions. They came to be known as Baptists.

The Puritans and the Anglicans tried to live together under one church. But with each passing decade doing so became more and more difficult. Other issues, especially economic, social, and political differences, figured prominently in the growing conflict.

The Reformation in Scotland

Protestantism arrived in Scotland very early, certainly by the mid-1520's. One of the earliest advocates of reform was Patrick Hamilton, a nobleman, humanist, and professor at Saint Andrews University. He was burned at the stake for heresy in 1528.

In 1542, King James V of Scotland died, leaving his daughter, Mary, as heir to the throne. Mary's mother ruled in the name of the child-queen and tried to bring Scotland under the control of her native France. The resistance to French influence brought together an alliance of Protestants and Scottish patriots.

The Protestants were scattered after an open rebellion against the Roman Catholics. John Knox (1513–1572), a leader of the cause, was sentenced to serve on a French ship, rowing with other prisoners.

After a year and a half the English government was able to obtain Knox's release from the French. But with French Roman Catholics in control in Scotland and

Mary Tudor ascending to the throne of England in 1553, Knox soon fled England for Geneva to sit at the feet of Calvin. Here he drank long and deep from Reformed Protestantism.

In 1559, the political situation in both France and Scotland had deteriorated. Knox returned in triumph to his native land and assumed leadership of the Protestant movement. With the help of England, in 1560 the Scottish Parliament made Protestantism the national religion.

Knox was a powerful preacher and an astute organizer. He guided Scottish Protestantism into a form of Calvinism known as Presbyterianism. The Scottish Reformation under Knox thoroughly united the church with a vision of patriotism. For many years most Scots believed that to be Scottish was to be Presbyterian and to defend Presbyterianism was to defend the homeland.

The Puritan Reformation

When Elizabeth died in 1603 after forty-five years on the throne, her cousin, James I (who was also James VI of Scotland) succeeded her. James meant new hope for the Puritans, for Presbyterian Calvinists in Scotland had raised him. Scottish Protestants had taken James from his mother, Mary, Queen of Scots.

What the Puritans did not know was that James had hated his upbringing. When he became king of England, he wanted to be able to enjoy the more "Roman Catholic" style of the Anglican church. Furthermore, he was determined to be obeyed; and he saw the Puritans as citizens who needed to learn obedience. In response to the Puritans' many demands, the only one to which he agreed was to authorize a new edition of the Bible in English. Thus we have the Authorized Version, or King James Version, of the Bible, published in 1611. This edition of the Bible was the result of a compromise between Puritans, Anglicans, and a Scottish king of England.

James and the Puritans had difficulty working

together. More and more of the members of Parliament came from the ranks of the rising middle class that was often Puritan in orientation. James I was followed on the throne by Charles I, his son.

Charles was even more determined than his father to be the absolute ruler of the realm. For eleven years he even tried to govern without Parliament. But a series of crises, foreign and domestic, forced him to call back Parliament, which had become not only heavily Puritan but militantly so. The road to the English Civil War was clear by 1642. Charles was beheaded in 1649; and England came under the control of Oliver Cromwell, a radical Protestant.

Charles II was able to restore the monarchy in 1660. By this time most Puritans had decided either to accept the church in its Anglican form or had left the church and suffered persecution for their faith.

The Reformation in England took much longer to come to a conclusion than was the case on the Continent. Part of that conclusion was a greater diversity and pluralism in religion than existed elsewhere.

During the time of the English Reformation, the English began colonizing the New World. Many of the issues of the English religious conflict found their way into the shaping of the American experiment. The Calvinism that fed the Puritans, encouraged the Separatists, and even influenced the Anglicans was the same form of religion that had led Dutch and French Protestants to seek certain political freedoms as a part of their quest for religious toleration. Calvinism, shaped by the events of history, contains many of the roots of modern democracy and religious liberty as well as the roots of contemporary understandings of the Christian faith.

The Reformation was an age of giants and great movements. How amazing that so much came out of a shy, intense child from the little town of Noyon in Picardy. God's choices are often surprising.